73443 EN
Teotihuacan: Designing an Ancient Mexican
City

George, Lynn
ATOS BL 6.2
Points: 0.5   MG

Teotihuacan
Designing an Ancient Mexican City

Calculating Perimeters and Areas of Squares and Rectangles

Lynn George

PowerMath™

The Rosen Publishing Group's
PowerKids Press™
New York

Published in 2004 by The Rosen Publishing Group, Inc.
29 East 21st Street, New York, NY 10010

Book Design: Michael J. Flynn

Photo Credits: Cover © Steve Vidler/SuperStock; p. 5 © Angelo Hornak/Corbis; pp. 9, 14, 29 © Gianni Dagli Orti/Corbis; p. 13 © Richard A. Cooke/Corbis; p. 19 © Yann Arthus-Bertrand/Corbis; p. 21 © Tibor Bognar/Corbis; p. 23 © Corbis; p. 25 © Randy Faris/Corbis; p. 27 © Fotos and Photos/Index Stock; p. 30 © Macduff Everton/Corbis.

Library of Congress Cataloging-in-Publication Data

George, Lynn.
  Teotihuacan : designing an ancient Mexican city : calculating
perimeters and areas of squares and rectangles / Lynn George.
       p. cm. — (PowerMath)
Includes index.
Summary: Demonstrates methods for calculating the perimeters and areas
of square and rectangles by exploring the ancient Mexican city of
Teotihuacan.
  ISBN 0-8239-8983-6 (lib. bdg.)
  ISBN 0-8239-8876-7 (pbk.)
  6-pack ISBN: 0-8239-7385-9
  1. Perimeters (Geometry)—Juvenile literature. 2. Area
measurement—Juvenile literature. 3. Teotihuacan Site (San Juan
Teotihuacan, Mexico)—Juvenile literature. [1. Perimeters (Geometry) 2.
Area measurement. 3. Teotihuacan Site (San Juan Teotihuacan, Mexico)]
I. Title. II. Series.
  QA465.G39 2004
  516—dc21
                                2003002126

Manufactured in the United States of America

Contents

About 30 miles northeast of Mexico City lie the **ruins** of a mysterious ancient city. We know that it was built about 2,000 years ago and flourished until around 750 A.D., when it was abandoned. However, no one knows who built the city, what they called it, or why they abandoned it.

When the **Aztecs** discovered the city many centuries later, they marveled at its beautiful structures and its regular **grid** plan. They believed it must be a sacred spot and named it Teotihuacan (tay-oh-tee-wah-KAHN), which means "place of the gods."

The people who built Teotihuacan must have had excellent math skills. The grid plan for the streets is uniform and orderly, and the structures were built with exact measurements. We can learn more about this ancient city by studying the perimeters and areas of the squares and rectangles created by its builders. The perimeter of a figure is the distance around its sides. The area is the space covered by the figure.

Teotihuacan was the first real city in the Americas. By around 500 A.D., between 125,000 and 200,000 people lived there. London, England, didn't have that many people until around 1600!

The Plan of Teotihuacan

Archaeologists have uncovered about 2,600 major structures at Teotihuacan. Among these are buildings that were used as temples, homes, workshops, and government offices. Most of the city's structures were enclosed within a rectangular area that was about 3 miles long and 2.75 miles wide. If you walked all the way around the rectangle of Teotihuacan, how far would you have walked? To find the answer, add the lengths of the 4 sides to get the perimeter.

```
  3.00  miles
  3.00  miles
  2.75  miles
+ 2.75  miles
 11.50  miles
```

The perimeter was about 11.5 miles.

What was the area covered by the rectangle? You can find the answer by multiplying the width of the rectangle (2.75 miles) by its length (3 miles).

```
  2.75  miles
x    3  miles
  8.25  square miles
```

Teotihuacan covered an area of about 8.25 square miles.

The main street of Teotihuacan was a straight, wide avenue that ran from south to north. The Aztecs called it the Avenue of the Dead, because they thought that the structures lining the avenue were **tombs**.

Pyramid of the Moon

Pyramid of the Sun

Avenue of the Dead

Merchants' Barrio

Atetelco (apartment building)

San Juan River

Citadel

Teotihuacan covered a larger area than ancient Rome, which was the capital of a great empire in Europe.

Great Compound

The rest of the city was laid out in relation to the Avenue of the Dead. On both sides of the avenue were smaller streets that ran **parallel** to the avenue. Other streets cut across these streets at right angles, creating Teotihuacan's regular grid of rectangular blocks. On average, the streets were 12 feet wide. All the streets were made of stucco. Stucco is a kind of plaster used to cover buildings made of bricks or stone.

A 1-story apartment building occupied each of the rectangular blocks in the city. Like the streets, these buildings were also made of stucco. There were about 2,000 apartment buildings in Teotihuacan. Each building had several apartments. Related families occupied the apartments in each building. This type of multifamily housing was unusual in Mexico. No other ancient Mexican civilization had such housing for its people.

This picture of stairs shows how the people of Teotihuacan constructed their buildings. The structures were made of rocks, which were then covered with stucco.

Living Space in Teotihuacan

The apartment buildings in Teotihuacan varied in size, as did the apartments in each building. A large building might have been about 200 feet long by about 175 feet wide. What is the perimeter of a large building like this? Add the lengths of the 4 sides to find the answer.

```
  200  feet
  200  feet
  175  feet
+ 175  feet
  750  feet
```

The perimeter of a large building was about 750 feet.

What was the area of this large building? You can find the answer by multiplying 175 feet by 200 feet.

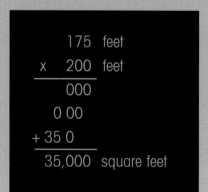

```
    175  feet
x   200  feet
    000
   0 00
+ 35 0
 35,000  square feet
```

The area of a large building was about 35,000 square feet.

Each apartment included living space, kitchens, rooms for sleeping, and places to worship. People were even buried under the floors of the apartments where they had lived!

rooms for sleeping

kitchens

living space

places to worship

entrance

The smallest apartment building in Teotihuacan was about 100 feet long and 70 feet wide. To find the perimeter of this building, add the lengths of its 4 sides.

```
100  feet
100  feet
 70  feet
+ 70  feet
340  feet
```

Now let's find the area of the smallest building. Multiply the length by the width to find the area.

```
    100  feet
x    70  feet
    ─────
    000
+ 7 00
  ─────────
  7,000  square feet
```

The area of this small building was about 7,000 square feet.

The living space allowed for each person was the same in all buildings. Around 100 people could live in a large building with 35,000 square feet. To figure out how much living space was allowed for each person, you would divide the number of square feet (35,000) by the number of people (100).

```
        350
   100)35,000
      - 300
      ─────
        500
      - 500
      ─────
         00
```

Each person was allowed about 350 square feet of living space.

To find out how many people could live in the smallest building, you would divide the total number of square feet in the building (7,000) by the number of square feet allowed for each person (350).

$$350 \overline{)\begin{array}{c} 20 \\ 7,000 \end{array}}$$
$$\underline{-\ 700}$$
$$00$$

About 20 people could live in the smallest building.

Walls in many of the apartment buildings were painted with colorful scenes. The paintings showed gods, people, animals, plants, mountains, water, and scenes of war.

On the west side of Teotihuacan was a medium-sized apartment building named Atetelco. This building was about 183 feet long and 115 feet wide. What was its perimeter? You can find the answer by adding the lengths of the 4 sides.

183	feet
183	feet
115	feet
+ 115	feet
596	feet

The perimeter of Atetelco was about 596 feet.

Tlaloc, the Rain God, decorates this clay dish. Tlaloc was one of the most important gods to the people of Teotihuacan because he brought rain, which made the crops grow and gave people water to drink. Images of Tlaloc decorated many objects in the city's homes.

What was the area of Atetelco? Multiply 183 feet by 115 feet to find the answer. An easy way to work a multiplication problem that involves 2 three-digit numbers is to break it into smaller parts. Since 115 = 100 + 15, first you can multiply 183 by 100. Next, multiply 183 by 15. Then add the answers to these 2 problems to get your final answer.

Step 1

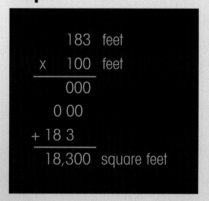

```
      183  feet
  x   100  feet
      000
    0 00
  + 18 3
   18,300  square feet
```

Step 2

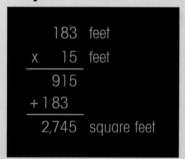

```
      183  feet
  x    15  feet
      915
  + 183
     2,745  square feet
```

Step 3

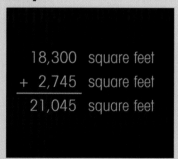

```
   18,300  square feet
  + 2,745  square feet
   21,045  square feet
```

Atetelco covered an area of about 21,045 square feet.

By around 200 A.D., Teotihuacan had become an important business and trading center that drew people from distant regions. Many of these people settled in the city, building neighborhoods with other people from their region who had also made homes in Teotihuacan. These people continued many of their old ways of doing things in their new city.

A community of traders grew up on the east side of Teotihuacan, next to the San Juan River. Because of the large number of traders in the area, archaeologists have named the district the Merchants' Barrio. Many people came from an area on Mexico's Gulf Coast that is near the modern city of Veracruz. They continued to build the kind of homes they were accustomed to, which were quite different from the usual homes in Teotihuacan. Rather than building rectangular apartment buildings, the immigrants from the region of Veracruz built round **adobe** houses with thatched roofs.

The homes built by the immigrants from Veracruz probably resembled the houses in this drawing.

The Avenue of the Dead

The Avenue of the Dead was the heart of Teotihuacan. The northern end of the avenue pointed toward a sacred mountain named Cerro Gordo (SEHR-oh GOHR-doh), which means "enormous hill." The avenue was about 2 miles long and about 50 yards wide. What was its perimeter? To find the answer, you must first have both measurements in the same **units**. It is easy to convert the length into yards. One mile equals 1,760 yards. How many yards are in 2 miles? Multiply 1,760 yards by 2 miles to find the answer.

1,760	yards per mile
x 2	miles
3,520	yards

Two miles are equal to 3,520 yards.

Now we can add the length, in yards, of all 4 sides to find the perimeter of the Avenue of the Dead.

3,520	yards
3,520	yards
50	yards
+ 50	yards
7,140	yards

The perimeter of the avenue is about 7,140 yards.

Avenue of the Dead

The width of the Avenue of the Dead was equal to half the length of a modern football field. The avenue was as long as 35 football fields placed end to end!

What was the area of the Avenue of the Dead? To find the answer, multiply the length by the width.

$$\begin{array}{r} 3{,}520 \text{ yards} \\ \times \quad 50 \text{ yards} \\ \hline 0\,000 \\ +176\,00 \\ \hline 176{,}000 \text{ square yards} \end{array}$$

The area of the avenue is about 176,000 square yards.

What if you wanted to give the area in square feet? There are 9 square feet in 1 square yard, so you would multiply 176,000 square yards by 9 square feet per square yard.

$$\begin{array}{r} 176{,}000 \text{ square yards} \\ \times \quad 9 \text{ square feet per square yard} \\ \hline 1{,}584{,}000 \text{ square feet} \end{array}$$

The area of the avenue is about 1,584,000 square feet!

Near the southern end of the avenue is the Great Compound, which was probably the city's main marketplace. On the other side of the avenue, opposite the Great Compound, was the **Citadel**. The Citadel got its name from the Spanish explorers who found the ruins of Teotihuacan in the 1500s. It may have been the city's center of government. Inside the Citadel were several palaces and temples.

The marketplace of the Great Compound probably looked much like the modern marketplace shown here.

The Citadel covered a square area that was about 1,300 feet on each side. What was its perimeter? There are 2 ways to solve this problem. You can add the lengths of the 4 sides, or you can multiply 1,300 feet by 4 sides.

Method 1

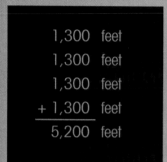

```
  1,300  feet
  1,300  feet
  1,300  feet
+ 1,300  feet
  5,200  feet
```

Method 2

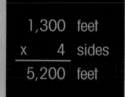

```
  1,300  feet
x     4  sides
  5,200  feet
```

Both methods give the same answer. The perimeter of the Citadel was about 5,200 feet. That's almost 1 mile!

The structures inside the Citadel included the **Pyramid** of the Feathered **Serpent**. The Feathered Serpent—also known as Quetzalcoatl (kwet-suhl-kuh-WAH-tuhl)—was the god of dawn, war, water, and agriculture.

The base of the Pyramid of the Feathered Serpent was a square that was about 220 feet on each side. What was the area of its base? You can multiply 220 feet by 220 feet to find the answer.

```
    220  feet
x  220  feet
---------
    000
   4 40
+ 44 0
---------
 48,400  square feet
```

The base of the pyramid covered an area of about 48,400 square feet. That's slightly more than 1 acre.

Many people now believe that the pyramid was the tomb of one of Teotihuacan's most powerful rulers. They have discovered several graves there, along with many valuable objects.

Around $\frac{3}{4}$ of a mile down the avenue from the Citadel is the Pyramid of the Sun. This pyramid was the second largest structure ever built in the ancient Americas. It was about 212 feet tall, or about the height of a 20-story building! Originally there was a temple on the top of the pyramid.

The pyramid's base was a square that was about 700 feet on each side. What was the perimeter of the base?

```
  700  feet
x    4  sides
-----------
2,800  feet
```

The Pyramid of the Sun's perimeter was about 2,800 feet. That's more than half a mile!

What was the area covered by the base of the pyramid? To find the answer, multiply 700 feet by 700 feet.

```
   700  feet
x  700  feet
-----------
   000
  000
+4900
-----------
490,000  square feet
```

The base of the Pyramid of the Sun covered an area of about 490,000 square feet.

Pyramid of the Sun

The base of the Pyramid of the Sun was about the same size as the base of the pyramid built around 2530 B.C. by the ancient Egyptian ruler named Khufu. It would take almost 10 football fields to cover the same area!

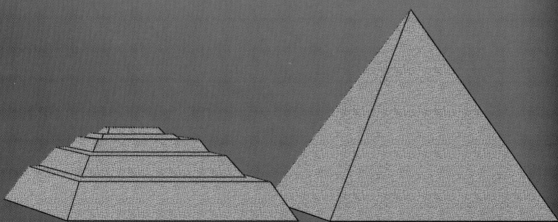

Pyramid of the Sun | Pyramid of Khufu

The Avenue of the Dead ends at the Pyramid of the Moon. If someone had stood in the middle of the avenue at the southern end and looked north, they would have been looking directly at the Pyramid of the Moon. Though this pyramid was smaller than the Pyramid of the Sun, its placement tells us that it must have had special meaning to the people of Teotihuacan.

The pyramid was about 140 feet tall. That's about the same height as a 14-story building. Like the Pyramid of the Sun, this pyramid originally had a temple on top. The pyramid's base was a square that was about 440 feet on each side. What was the area covered by the pyramid? To find the area of a square, multiply the length of 1 side by the length of another side.

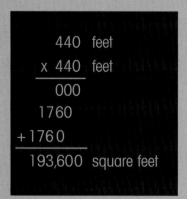

```
   440   feet
 x 440   feet
 ─────
   000
  1760
+1760
 ──────
 193,600   square feet
```

The base of the Pyramid of the Moon covered an area of about 193,600 square feet.

If someone stood in front of the Pyramid of the Moon and faced south, with the pyramid at their back, they would have been looking straight down the middle of the Avenue of the Dead.

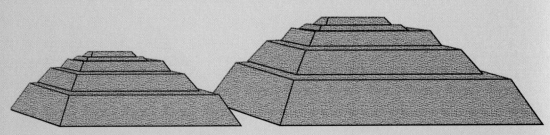

Pyramid of the Moon　　　　**Pyramid of the Sun**

In front of the Pyramid of the Moon was the **Plaza** of the Moon. Around the edges of the plaza were several smaller pyramids. Each of these originally had a temple on top. Right in front of the Pyramid of the Moon was a small building that had 10 altars inside. There was also a large platform in the middle of the plaza. The priests of Teotihuacan would have used the altars and platform for religious **ceremonies**.

The Plaza of the Moon was a square with sides that were about 600 feet long. What was the perimeter of the plaza? Multiply 600 feet by 4 sides to find the answer.

```
  600   feet
x     4   sides
  2,400   feet
```

The plaza's perimeter was about 2,400 feet. That's almost half of a mile!

What was the area of the plaza? To find the answer, multiply 600 feet by 600 feet.

```
    600  feet
x   600  feet
   ------
    000
   000
+ 3600
  ------
360,000  square feet
```

The Plaza of the Moon covered an area of about 360,000 square feet.

Although they have lost their temples, the small pyramids around the Plaza of the Moon still exist. The platform in the middle of the plaza also remains.

Pyramid of the Sun

Plaza of the Moon

Pyramid of the Moon

The Meaning of Math

The people who built Teotihuacan believed that there was order and reason in the universe. They wanted their society to be in harmony with the order in the universe. They believed that to accomplish this, their city had to be laid out very carefully. The size and placement of important structures had to be measured exactly. Even the city streets had to be organized into a regular grid. The people of Teotihuacan developed excellent math skills so they could accomplish their goals. For these people, math was what made it possible to live in harmony with the universe. It was one of the most important skills in their civilization.

Glossary

adobe (uh-DOH-bee) A word describing blocks of mud and straw that have been dried in the sun.

archaeologist (ar-kee-AH-luh-jist) A scientist who uses ancient objects and buildings to study what life was like in the past.

Aztec (AZ-tek) A member of the group of Indians who ruled much of Mexico from 1428 to the 1520s.

ceremony (SAIR-uh-moh-nee) An event to honor the importance of something, often with music, dancing, and prayer.

citadel (SIH-tuh-duhl) A castle that commands a great city.

grid (GRIHD) The pattern formed by a group of evenly spaced lines that have another group of evenly spaced lines cutting across them at right angles.

parallel (PAIR-uh-lehl) Running side by side and always staying the same distance apart.

plaza (PLA-zuh) A public square in a city or town.

pyramid (PEER-uh-mid) A large structure that usually has a square base and 4 sloping sides that meet in a point or a platform at the top.

ruins (ROO-uhnz) Buildings that have fallen apart or been destroyed.

serpent (SUHR-puhnt) Another name for a snake.

tomb (TOOM) A building where the dead are buried.

unit (YOU-nuht) A standard quantity used for measurement.

Index